Animals
of the Forest

by Emma Rattenbury

Harcourt
SCHOOL PUBLISHERS

Cover ©Photolibrary.com; 2 ©Alamy Images; 3ñ8 ©Photolibrary.com

Printed in the United States of America

ISBN 10: 0-15-350628-8
ISBN 13: 978-0-15-350628-4

Ordering Options
ISBN 10: 0-15-350598-2 (Grade 1 On-Level Collection)
ISBN 13: 978-0-15-350598-0 (Grade 1 On-Level Collection)
ISBN 10: 0-15-357785-1 (package of 5)
ISBN 13: 978-0-15-357785-7 (package of 5)

3 4 5 6 7 8 9 10   179   15 14 13 12 11 10 09 08

Many kinds of animals live in this forest. They all have many things that help them live.

Beavers

Beavers only live in or near water. In the water, a clear skin slides across their eyes. How does this skin help?

Beavers swim a lot. The clear skin keeps things out of their eyes when they are in the water.

Beavers make their homes out of sticks and mud.

Eagles

An eagle can see very well. It has eyes on the side of its head. How do eyes on the side of its head help?

An eagle can see to the front and to the side at the same time. This helps it spot small animals when it is hunting. It uses its eyes to see how far away an animal is. It can see in color, too.

Star-nosed Moles

This mole has a nose that looks like a star. There is no hair on it. How does a star nose help?

The mole's nose has little arms. The arms help it find food. The mole uses its toes to dig. The arms help keep things from going up its nose.

Good-bye, mole!